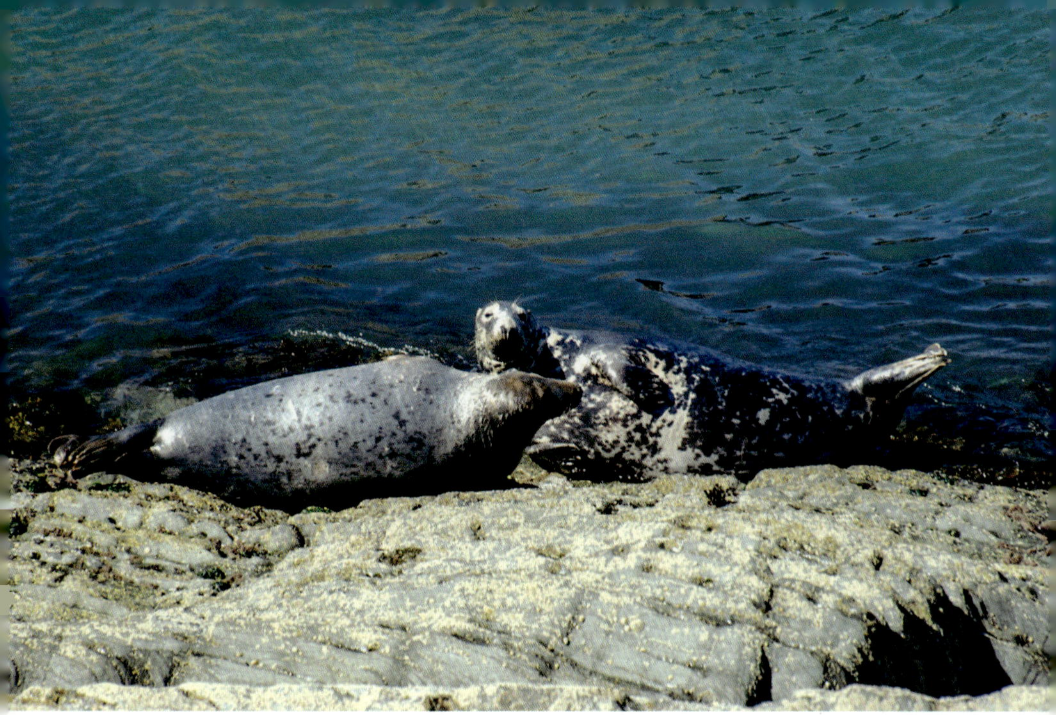

Fairly Easy Walks
in North Devon

Robert Hesketh

Bossiney Books

All the walks in this book were checked prior to publication, at which time the instructions were correct. However, changes can occur in the countryside over which neither the author nor the publisher has any control. Please let us know if you encounter any serious problems.

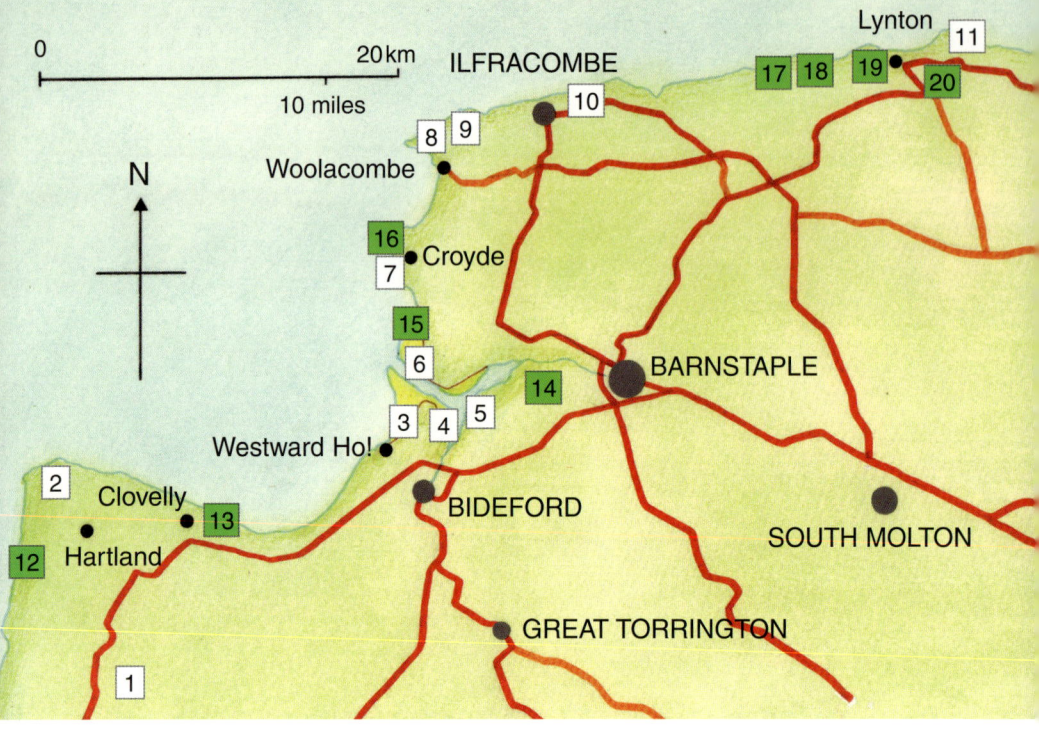

The approximate starting points of the walks in this book. Walks 1-11 are 'circular', walks 12-20 are 'there-and-back' walks. West of Bideford and east of Ilfracombe the North Devon coast is decidedly hilly: in these areas there-and-back walks are often the best way to see the dramatic coastal scenery without encountering steep ascents and descents.

First published 2019 by
Bossiney Books Ltd, 67 West Busk Lane, Otley, LS21 3LY
www.bossineybooks.com

© 2019 Robert Hesketh All rights reserved
ISBN 978-1-906474-75-1

Acknowledgements
The maps are by Graham Hallowell.
All photographs are by the author, www.roberthesketh.co.uk

Printed in Great Britain by R Booth Ltd, Penryn, Cornwall

Introduction

The routes in this book are chosen to help you explore the easier side of North Devon walking. Most are from 2.5 km/1 1/2 miles up to 5.4 km/3 1/2 miles, with one of 7.9 km/5 miles. Some routes are a little more challenging than others, so the time needed to complete them will vary too. If you're out of practice, try starting with the easiest walks and build stamina as you go. Why hurry? There are many wonderful viewpoints and places of interest to linger over on the way. Walking is a safe and healthy exercise, but please watch out for uneven ground and unfenced cliffs.

Footwear and clothing

Walking is a pleasure throughout the seasons so long as you are prepared. There will be some mud at most times of the year and perhaps a lot of mud and puddles in winter. Walking boots are ideal, but sandals inadequate, whilst Wellingtons don't breathe or provide ankle support.

   North Devon's weather can change suddenly and rainfall is above the average for England, so it's wise to bring extra layers of clothing as well as a waterproof. On some paths there may be gorse or nettles, so trousers are preferable to shorts; they also provide some protection against ticks which may carry Lyme disease. If a tick does attach itself to you, remove it promptly and carefully with tweezers.

Extras

Drinking water is a must – you will soon need it and dehydration causes tiredness. I recommend a walking pole or stick too and a mobile phone. The sketch maps in this book are just that – sketches. You may want to carry an OS Explorer map for extra information.

The countryside

Despite many pressures on their livelihoods, farmers are still trying to make a living from the land you will pass through. Please respect their livestock and don't feed the ponies on the Exmoor and Northam walks as it encourages them onto the roads. Leave gates closed or open as you find them, and keep dogs under control, especially during the lambing and bird nesting season.

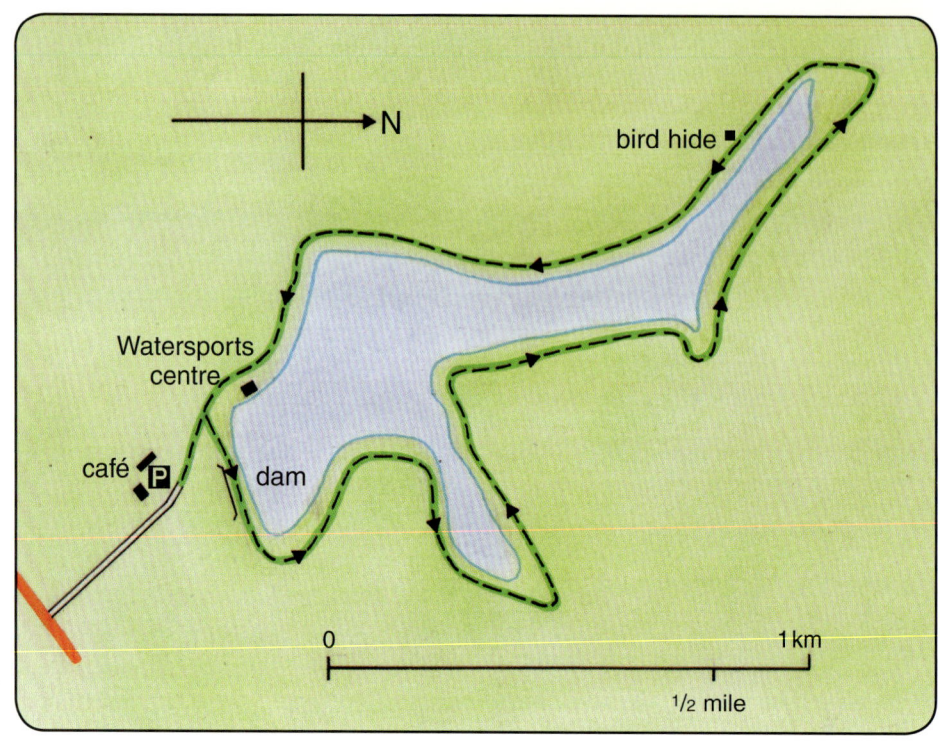

Walk 1 Upper Tamar Lake

Distance: 5.2km/3¼ miles
Character: This easy walk offers views of the Upper Tamar Lake and the pleasant rolling green fields beyond from all angles.

It follows a broad, well surfaced and mainly level path, which is suitable for pushchairs, wheelchairs and bikes. Take binoculars – it is a great place to watch a variety of waterfowl and woodland birds too.

The Tamar Lakes are signed from Kilkhampton on the A39. Start at the Upper Lake car park, where there is a helpful map and information plaques opposite the café (open all year) and toilets. Turn left and then right across the dam, LAKESIDE WALK. Turn left again (LAKESIDE WALK) at the far side of the dam.

Navigation from this point could not be easier: simply follow the path around the lake for nearly 5km (3 miles). Just before reaching the boathouse, the path divides. Keep right as signed and follow the path behind the boathouse to the start.

Cormorant

Stone chat

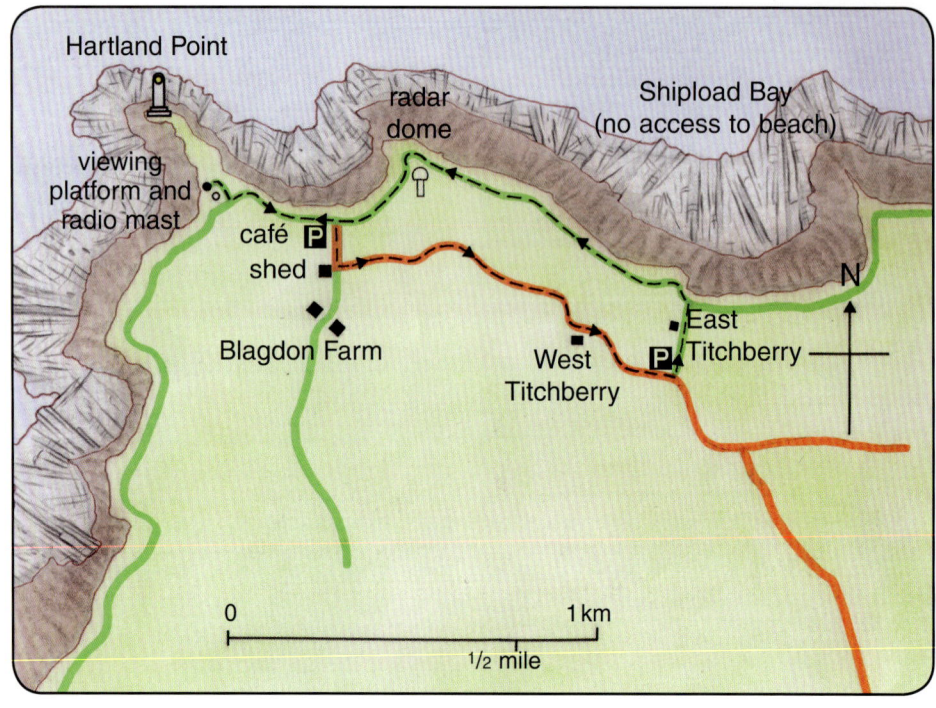

Walk 2   East Titchberry and Hartland Point

Distance: 3.8 km (2½ miles)
Character: This dramatically beautiful walk is surprisingly gentle. The Point, with its high cliffs and lighthouse, is at the junction between the Atlantic and the Bristol Channel. Low tide reveals the 'Johanna', one of a long line of wrecks; she came to grief in 1982.

Park in the National Trust's car park at East Titchberry, beside the road out towards Hartland Point. From the top end of the car park, turn left (COAST PATH BRIDLEWAY) passing the farmhouse to your left. Turn left at the coast path, HARTLAND POINT.

Walk round the enclosure of the mushroom-shaped radar dome. Built in 1994, this is the successor to the RAF's Hartland radar station, which plotted shipping and aircraft during the Second World War and for some time afterwards.

Arriving at the Hartland Point café and car park, continue ahead, COAST PATH HARTLAND QUAY, towards the Point. Whilst there is a path of sorts to the rocky end of the point, it is difficult and risky, so we don't recommend it. There is a viewing point with a helpful information board, from which to look over the wild seascape.

Retrace your steps to the café. Turn right and follow the tarmac track past the Lundy heliport. Turn left (PUBLIC BRIDLEWAY) and walk past the wooden hut. Follow the lane past West Titchberry to the starting point.

Hartland Point is a landmark for migrating birds, making visits in Autumn and Spring particularly interesting. Resident species include ravens, peregrines and (especially) buzzards.

The Point is also a favourite place for seals, which are most vocal in the breeding season, from September to December. Their calls, somewhere between a bark and a trumpet blast, are large and exuberant, like their generous waistlines. Mature males grow to over 2 m long and weigh in at well over 200 kg. Females average a modest 155 kg.

Hartland light was built in 1874 and manned until 1984. Alas, it did not save every vessel on this busy sea lane from running into the rocks, as *Johanna's* rusting carcass testifies. All her crew were safely brought to land by the rescue services, but they were less than pleased when the *Johanna's* cargo was later brought ashore – by looters.

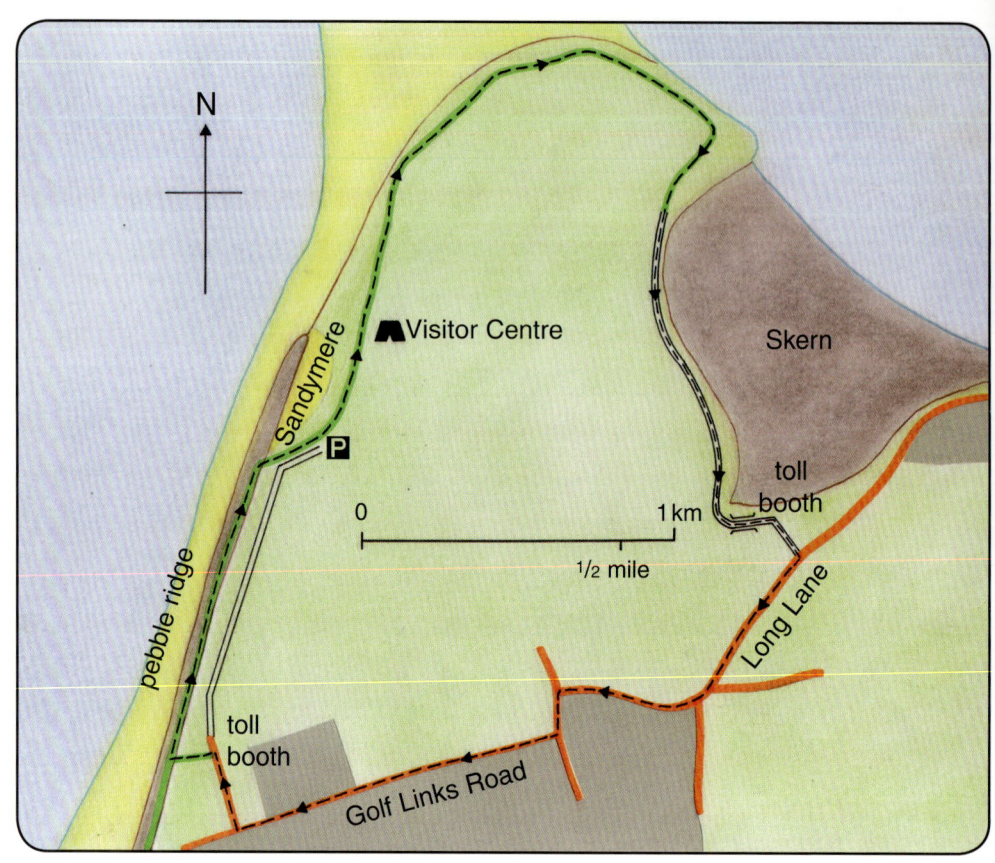

Walk 3 Northam Burrows

Distance: 7.9km/5 miles
Character: This almost entirely level walk follows the Coast Path around the perimeter of Northam Burrows Country Park, 253ha (607 acres) of dunes, salt marsh and coastal grassland noted for its birds. The views across Sandymere beach and the Taw/Torridge estuary are vast.
Please note that dogs must be kept on leads and have restricted access to the beach.

Drive up the toll road from Westward Ho! and park behind Sandymere near the Visitor Centre. Follow the path to the Visitor Centre. Continue north on the sandy path around the perimeter of the golf course. Turn right at a fingerpost. Continue in the same direction around the Skern, a huge area of mud flats and salt marsh.

Turn left over the bridge. Cross the cattle grid and continue ahead on the lane. Reaching a junction, turn right into LONG LANE. Continue along the pavement when Long Lane merges into a street. Reaching a junction, turn left, NORTHAM BIDEFORD. Turn right into GOLF LINKS ROAD.

Turn right into PEBBLERIDGE ROAD, signed NORTHAM BURROWS. Continue to the toll booth. From here, you may simply follow the tarred track ahead to the start, but more interesting and scenic alternatives are to follow the pebble ridge from the duck boards opposite the toll booth (if the tide is in), or to walk along the beach (if the tide is out – please observe dog restrictions).

Continue until you reach the duck boards at the southern end of Sandymere. Leave the pebble ridge and follow the track behind Sandymere to the start.

> Ponies and sheep graze on on the coastal grassland that makes up half the area of Northam Burrows, which used to be a common for the local 'potwallopers' – cottagers who had a vote pre-1832, on the grounds that they had their own hearth on which to boil a pot.

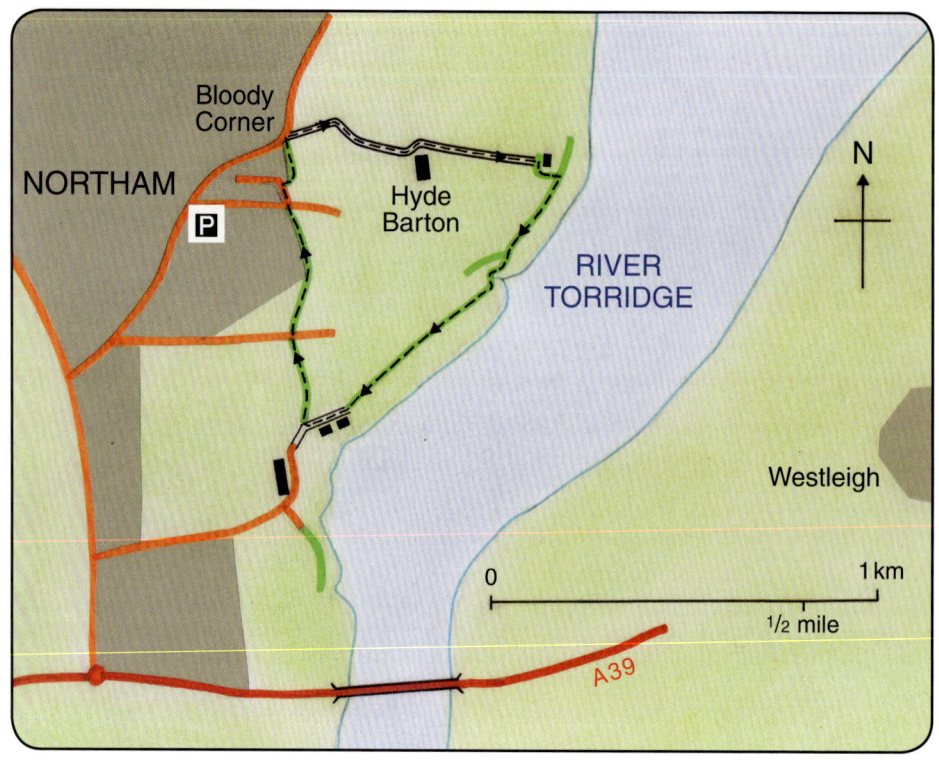

Walk 4 Bloody Corner, Northam

Distance:: 2.5 km (1 1/2 miles)

Character: This fairly gentle walk mainly by riverbank and field paths offers splendid views of the river Torridge. It starts from a probable battle site of 878, when Devon men defeated a Viking host.

Getting there: From the roundabout on the A39 at Bideford, take the Northam road. After 0.7 km (nearly half a mile) turn right, APPLEDORE. Bloody Corner is 0.8 km (half a mile) towards Appledore, where the grass verge on the left broadens considerably. Park carefully by the roadside, or if there is no space, use the Windmill Lane car park 200 m back up the hill on the left.

From the Bloody Corner memorial take the tarred track ahead, a public footpath, HYDE BARTON. Follow the twists past Hyde Barton as far as a wooden gate signed BOAT HYDE AND THE MOORINGS.

Turn right through a gate, COAST PATH. This path leads to the riverbank, with good views of Westleigh and of Instow further downriver. Look out for and listen for wading birds.

Turn right and follow the path for about 200m, then turn left (acorn sign, NATIONAL TRUST BOROUGH FARM).

Follow the bankside path over a small creek by duckboards. (If the tide is in, there is an alternative higher path which soon rejoins the main path.) Continue along a fenced section, with views up-river to the new road bridge and beyond.

Just before the track descends to the valley bottom, turn sharp right through a gate, PUBLIC FOOTPATH. Walk uphill past a tree plantation. Cross a tarmac track and through a gate, continuing on the footpath with the hedge on your left. Do not turn into the housing estate, but continue along the fenced footpath to a street.

Turn left and immediately right down GREENACRE CLOSE, enjoying the sea view. After 50m, turn right (PUBLIC FOOTPATH) at a metal gate, then turn left down the field edge to a metal gate at the bottom left corner. Turn left back to Bloody Corner.

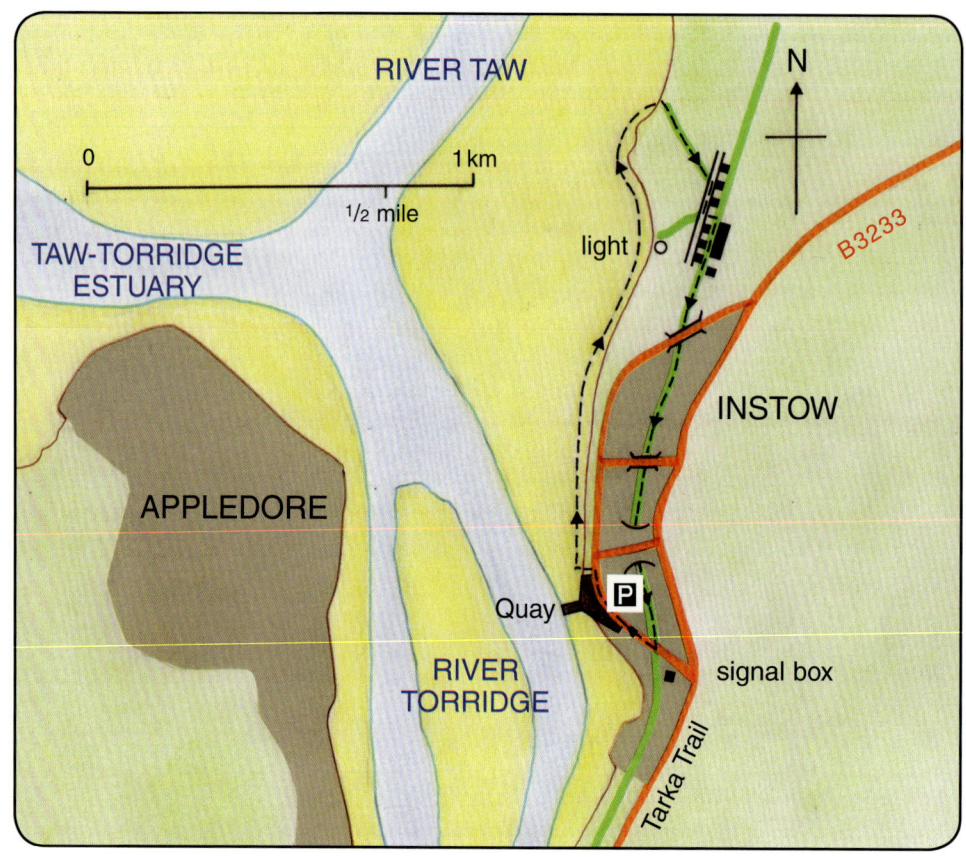

Walk 5 Instow

Distance: 3 km (2 miles) – less if you use the high tide short cut. Character: A beautiful walk along Instow's sandy beach, with views across the estuary to Appledore and Braunton Burrows, is followed by an easy return along the Tarka Trail. Here the former railway line has been smoothly surfaced and is pushchair-friendly. The whole route is level.

From the signed car park on Instow's Marine Parade, turn right. After 75 m, leave the pavement at the beach kiosk and follow the top edge of the beach. Continue along the beach leaving Instow behind you and keeping the dunes on your right.

On reaching the navigation light, you may wish to take a short cut on the right across MOD property and along the concrete

track to a former level crossing. If the tide is very high, you may be obliged to do this, in which case ignore the next paragraph.

Otherwise, continue ahead with the sea wall on your right until you reach the COAST PATH sign. Turn right up the steps onto the sea wall. Leaving the Coast Path, continue ahead (PUBLIC FOOTPATH) past a cricket ground and thatched pavilion. Turn right along a metalled track past wooden chalets as far as the MOD concrete road and turn left.

Turn right at the former level crossing onto the Tarka Trail – beware cyclists! Continue to Instow signal box, which dates from 1872 and is a listed building. Preserved along with its levers, and short section of re-laid track and a working signal, it is open on Sunday afternoons.

Turn right and follow Marine Parade back to the car park.

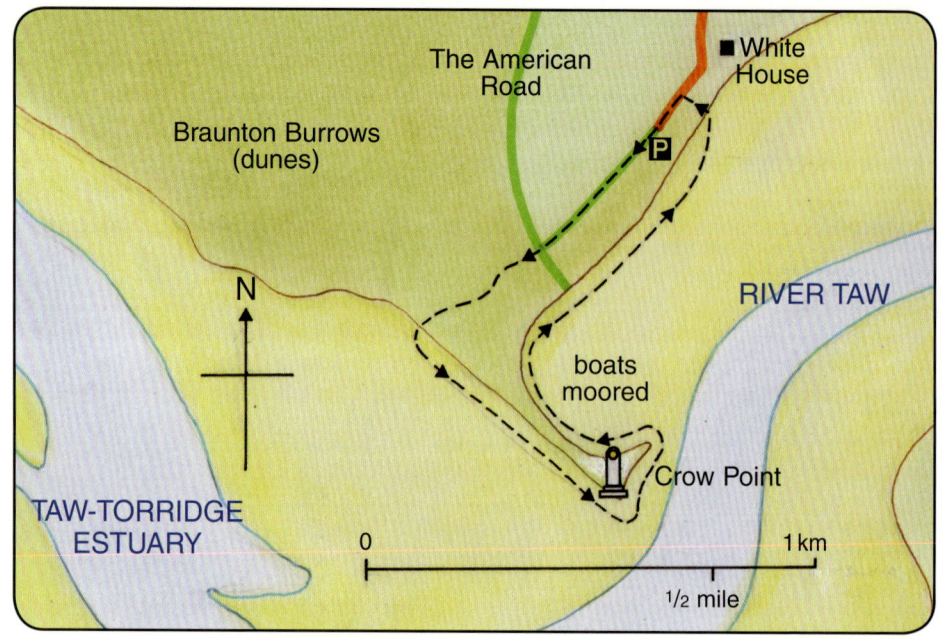

Walk 6 Crow Point and Braunton Burrows

Distance: 4km (2½ miles)

Character: A level and entirely off-road walk with impressive views from the massive sand-dunes of Braunton Burrows to North Devon's Atlantic coast and the Taw-Torridge estuary. The Burrows' remarkable variety of wildflowers and birds provide added interest.

Getting there: From Braunton take the road signed to Crow Point. The latter part is a toll road, but with a modest toll and free parking.

Leave Crow Point car park from the western end (furthest from the toll road). Take the path between two large boulders beside a notice board which gives information on the Burrows' flora and fauna.

Stay on the path when it crosses a rough track – the 'American Road'. (US troops trained in this area of north Devon as well as at Slapton on the south coast in preparation for D-Day, 1944.) Please stay on the duckboards to minimise erosion and damage to plants.

Arriving at the beach, turn left and walk along to Crow Point. Try to find the hardest sand to make the going easier! From Crow Point's red navigation light (private property belonging to Trinity House) follow the beach around the hook-shaped Point, keeping to the sand to avoid the sticky mud closer to the water line.

A variety of boats are moored in the lee of Crow Point. Ahead is the White House. Built for the marsh keeper, it was formerly known as Ferry House because a ferry ran from here to Appledore until 1939.

As you approach the White House, look out for a flight of metal steps. These lead back to the car park.

Braunton Burrows is a UNESCO Biosphere Reserve, renowned for its great diversity and wealth of flora. Over 400 species of flowering plants have been recorded here. The Burrows also support a strong butterfly population, whilst skylarks, whitethroats and stonechats are common. Look out for waders and heron on the marshes.

Warning
The Burrows are still used for military training. Although this does not directly affect this walk, do not pick up metal objects or enter areas of the Burrows marked off with red flags – which implies live firing.

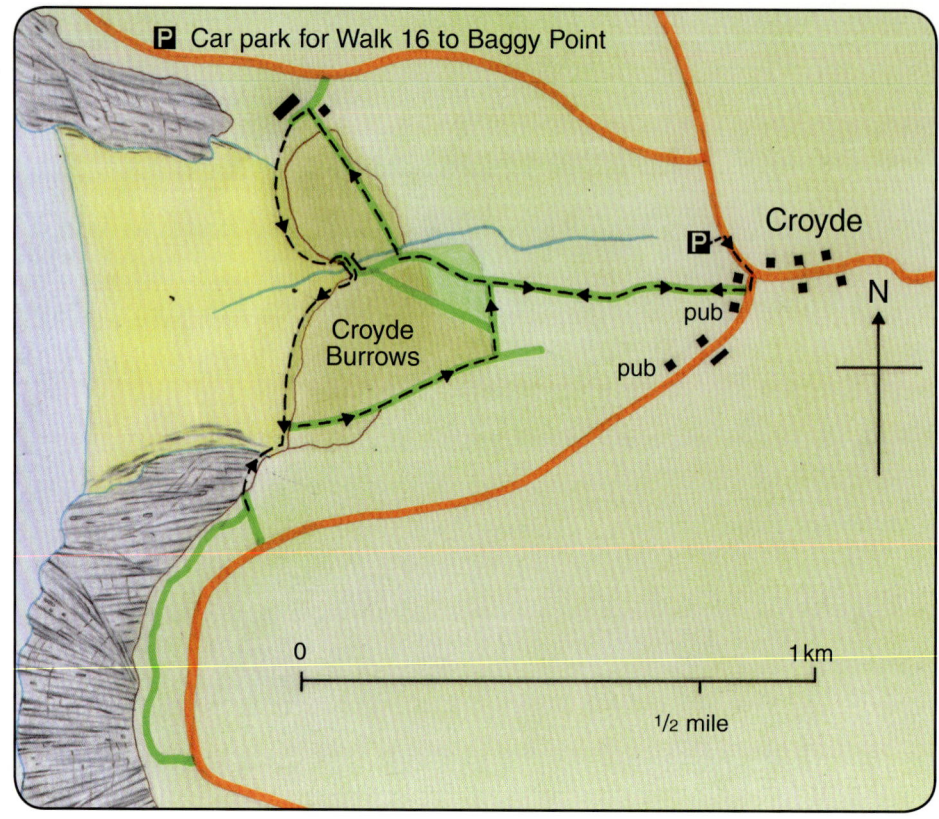

Walk 7 Croyde Burrows

Distance: 4km (2½ miles)

Character: Salt air and the roar of surf are the usual companions on this invigorating exploration of Croyde's large golden beach and sand dunes. The route is almost entirely off road and involves no steep slopes.

Start from Croyde's village hall car park. Turn right out of the car park and right again at Billy Budd's pub. Stay on the enclosed path until you reach a small meadow. Bear diagonally right.

Do not take the first path right, into the caravan park. Take the second right over a footbridge and into the dunes. Please stay with the path to minimise erosion and avoid adders, which like to bask in quiet spots on the sand. Dogs should be kept to the path.

On reaching the beach café, turn left and walk along the top edge of the beach – part of the official Coast Path – to a stream. Follow

it inland to a footbridge and cross. Make your way along the far side of the stream and continue along the beach to a ramp at the far end. This leads through a cove to public steps at the far end of the beach. Climb these for superb views of Baggy Point and of the saw-toothed rocks leading to it.

   Now return to the ramp and retrace your steps along the beach for 100 m. Turn right at a wooden fingerpost and walk up the dune to a large metal signboard. Continue inland along the sandy path through the dunes and past chalets to a junction of paths. Turn left. At the next path junction turn right, cross the meadow and retrace your steps to the start.

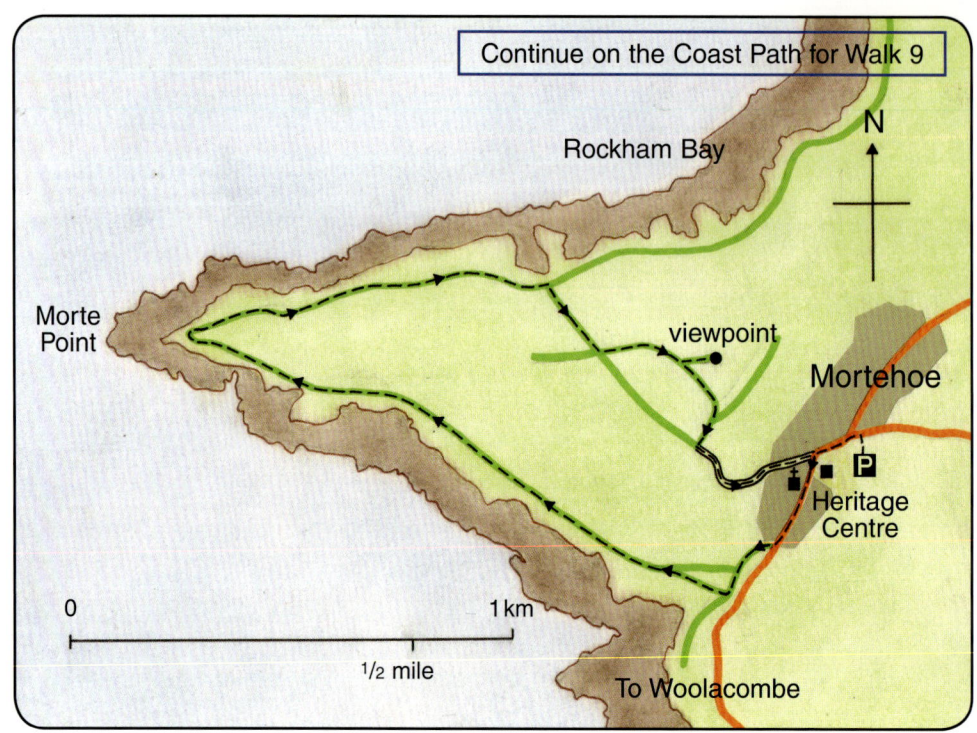

Walk 8 Mortehoe and Morte Point

Distance: 4km (2½ miles)
Character: Choose a clear day for this stimulating coastal walk: the views are superb, especially from Morte Point with its dramatic slate formations – which have proved fatal for many ships. Watch out for seals, often seen basking on the rocks (see title page) and beware of uneven footing around Morte Point.
If you feel energetic, you can extend this walk to include Walk 9.

Turn left out of Mortehoe car park. Follow the lane as it curves left past the church. Continue past the Chichester Arms and downhill. Ignore the first footpath on your right. Turn right through a gate at the next signed path. Follow the grassy path downhill.

Turn right onto the Coast Path. When it divides, keep to the lower path (the official Coast Path) and follow it around Morte Point. Continue east towards Bull Point for 900m, ignoring side turnings.

If you want to join Walk 9, continue ahead on the Coast Path. Otherwise turn right (MORTEHOE) up a broad grassy path for 250 m. Turn left through a gap in the low wall on a broad uphill path. Turn left again at the fingerpost, VIEWPOINT. Retrace your steps to the VIEWPOINT fingerpost and turn left. Reaching a stone wall, bear right and follow the grassy path downhill.

Turn left at the path junction and follow the track through gates. Continue on the lane ahead into Mortehoe. Retrace your steps to the car park, past the aptly named 'Ship Aground'.

> The anchor in the pub garden belonged to SS *Collier*, wrecked at Rockham Bay in 1914. There, the ship's boiler can still be seen on the beach at low tide by diverting down the steps in Walk 9. For more information about Mortehoe's maritime history, visit the excellent museum next to the car park

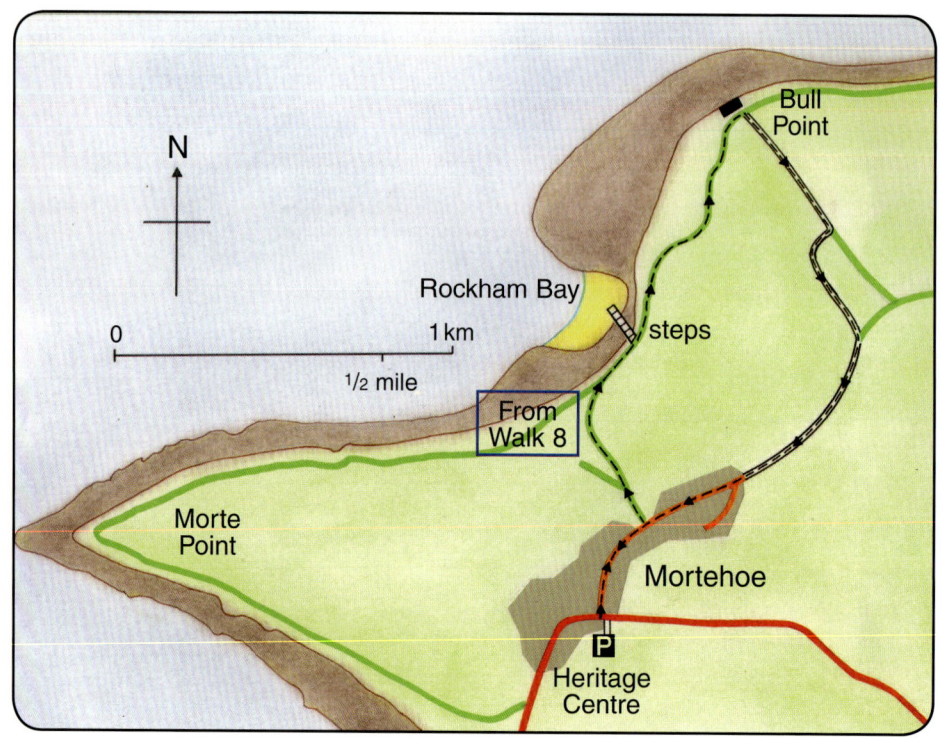

Walk 9   Mortehoe and Bull Point

Distance: 4.1km (2½ miles)
Character: An exhilarating coastal walk with splendid views. There are some steep, but short slopes.

Leave Mortehoe car park. Take the lane ahead, LIGHTHOUSE LEE. Turn left, ROCKHAM BEACH. Follow the path downhill. Continue ahead at a path junction, ROCKHAM BEACH.

Turn right onto the Coast Path. Continue ahead at Rockham, or divert left down the steps to visit the beach itself, where the boiler from SS *Collier* is visible at low tide. If you do this, please beware of incoming tides and that the cliffs may be unstable.

Follow the Coast Path to Bull Point.

Turn right (MORTEHOE) when you reach the entrance to Bull Point lighthouse and follow the tarred path ahead, ignoring side turnings. Reaching a tarred lane, keep right and walk ahead. Retrace your steps to the start from the path to Rockham Beach.

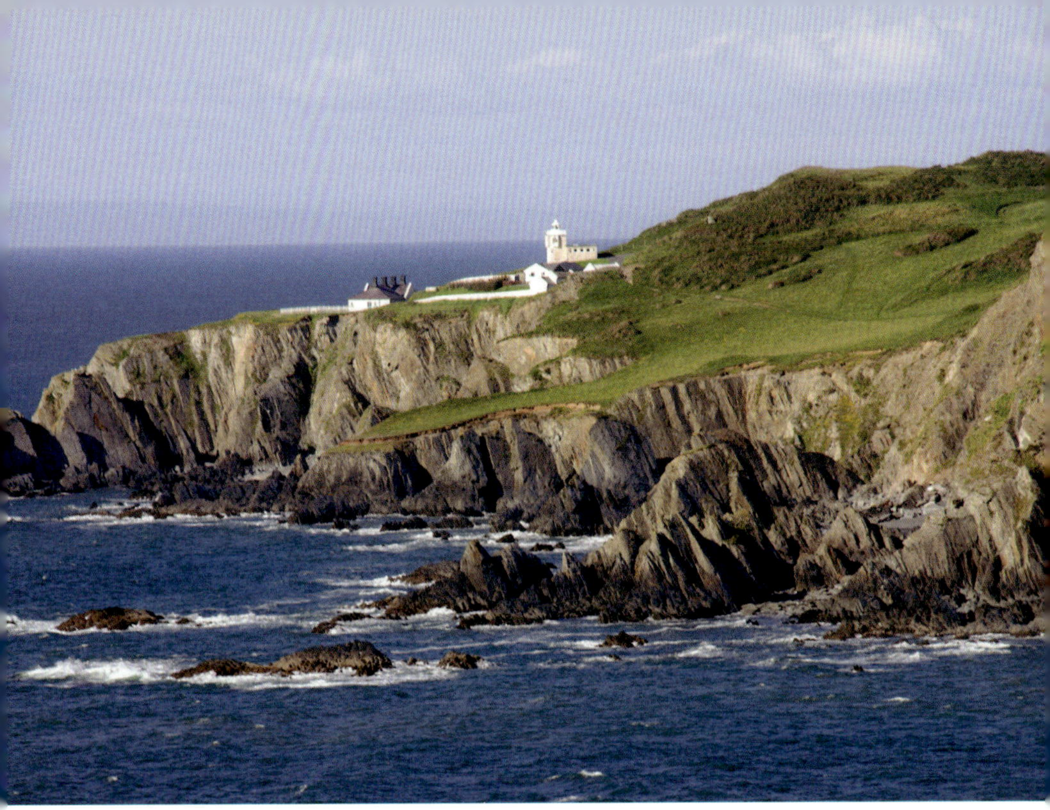

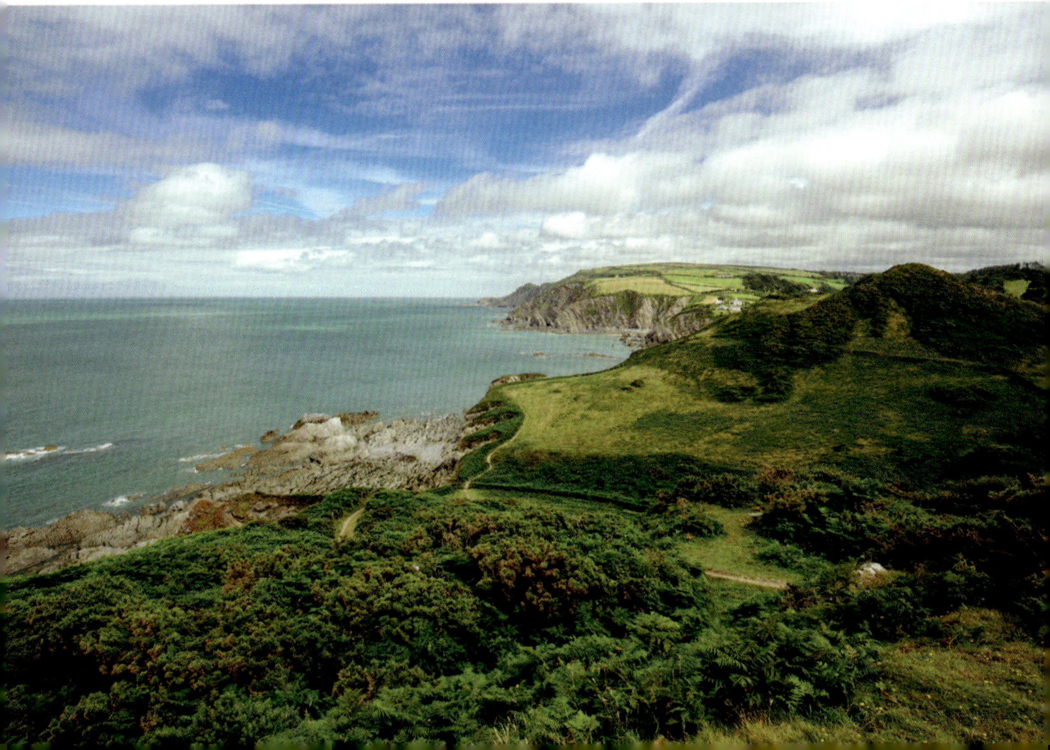

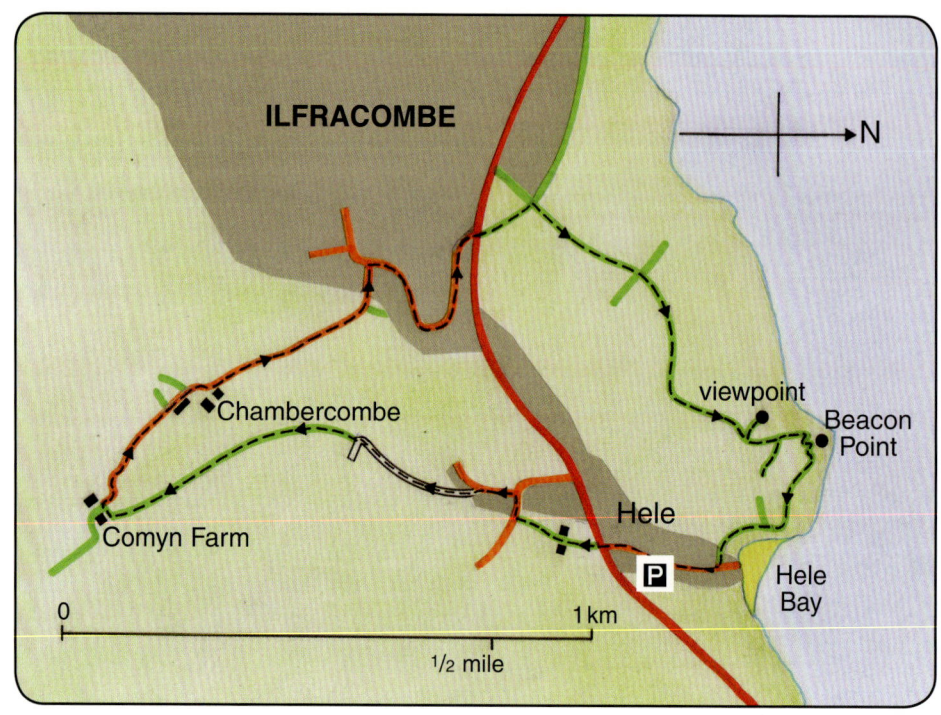

Walk 10 Hele and Chambercombe

Distance: 4km (2½ miles)
Character: This rewarding walk includes superb views of Ilfracombe, the coast, and Devon's chequerboard of green fields. It also passes Hele Mill and Chambercombe Manor, both well worth a visit. There is one long ascent and one long descent.

Turn left out of Hele Bay car park. Cross the main road carefully and take the PUBLIC FOOTPATH opposite, to Hele Mill. Continue on the footpath to a tarmac lane. Turn right, follow the lane around the bend and keep left, COMYN TRAYNE. At Witheridge Place, turn left up a tarmac track. Walk uphill to a left bend: take the PUBLIC FOOTPATH straight ahead at this point, which leads to Comyn Farm.

Entering the farmyard, turn right and right again, PUBLIC BRIDLEWAY ILFRACOMBE. Walk along this tarmac track or lane to Chambercombe Manor, then for a further 400m. Stay on the lane as it curves left to a road junction. Turn right, and follow the street as it winds round, then descends to the main road.

Cross carefully and take the tarmac path to the left of the swimming pool. After passing the pool turn right and follow the tarmac path uphill to another junction. Continue ahead, COAST PATH TO HELE BAY, and climb to the highest point on this section of the Coast Path. Divert left to the viewpoint and information board on the summit (114m).

Retrace your steps to the Coast Path and turn left. Ignore the turn right. Continue to an old viewing platform. Follow the zig-zag Coast Path downhill as signed. Turn right at the beach, back up the road to the car park.

> Hele Mill (limited seasonal opening) is mentioned in documents of 1525, but the present corn mill is of unknown age. Derelict after 1945, it was restored in the 1970s and is now run as a working museum, which mills its own flour. It has an attractive tea garden.
>
> Chambercombe Manor's tearooms and beautiful gardens (donations) are open to the public, as are the woodland walks. It began as a medieval open hall house and has been continuously occupied over the centuries. There are fascinating guided tours, introducing visitors to the chequered and sometimes tragic past of Chambercombe, and the ghosts said to haunt it.

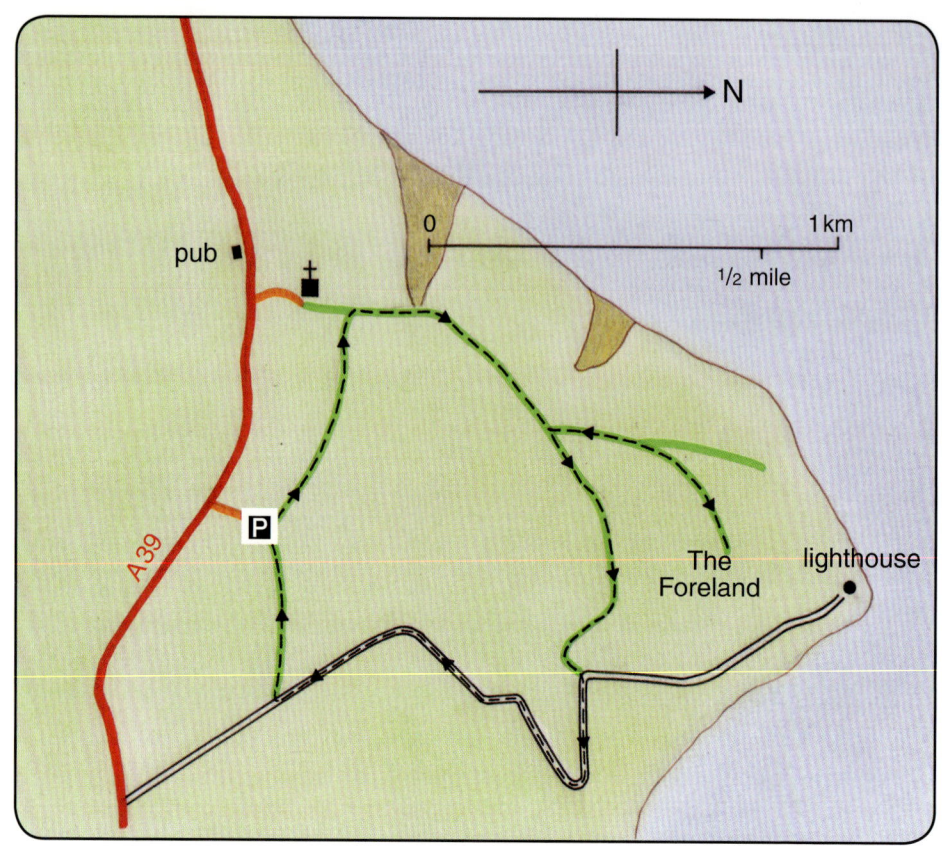

Walk 11 Countisbury

Distance: 5.4 km (3½ miles)
Character: Standing 210 m above the sea with dramatic scree slopes, Countisbury's Foreland offers magnificent views east and west to a succession of Exmoor's highest cliffs and across the sea to Wales. This walk includes one long steady descent and ascent.

Begin at Barna Barrow car park. With your back to the road, turn left and follow the stone wall on your left.

Divert left if you wish to visit the church, or the medieval Blue Ball Inn, with its cavernous fireplace, bread oven and cooking jacks. Retrace your steps to the church.

Leave by the north gate of the church and follow the Coast Path north along the contour of the cliff. Continue ahead at the next path junction, COAST PATH PORLOCK.

From the next fingerpost, continue to the crest of the hill ahead for the best views. Retrace your steps to the fingerpost and turn left, COAST PATH PORLOCK. Follow the Coast Path downhill to a tarred lane.

Turn right and follow the lane uphill. When it curves sharp right, leave the Coast Path. Continue following the lane as it zig-zags uphill. Turn right onto the footpath, LYNMOUTH. When the path divides, keep left and continue to the start.

Walk 12 Speke's Mill Mouth

The 1.25 km (1 mile) of Coast Path between Hartland Quay and the South West Coast Path's largest waterfall at Speke's Mill Mouth offers some of Devon's most spectacular coastal scenery in return for a fairly modest effort. The vista along the cliffs and far into Cornwall is stunning. On the way you will see marvellous rock formations, both in the cliffs and in the rocky beaches below, especially at Speke's Mill Mouth, accessed by steps.

Walk 13 Clovelly and The Hobby Drive

Follow the tarred path downhill from the Clovelly Visitor Centre. Either continue downhill TO THE VILLAGE, or turn right, HOBBY DRIVE. The Hobby Drive is broad, level and well surfaced, having been, built as a carriage drive. It winds for nearly 5 km (3 miles) through woodland rich in wild flowers and offers pleasing glimpses of the coast. Clovelly village should not be missed – it is exceptionally beautiful and interesting. Cars are banned from its steep, narrow cobbled streets, where the closely packed cottages are preserved as much as possible as they would have been in the mid 19th century. Continue to the harbour, from where there is a regular Land Rover service back to the car park.

The old railway bridge at Fremington Quay

Walk 14 Fremington Quay

Follow the signs for FREMINGTON QUAY from the B3223. From the car park, head west along the Tarka Trail to the Fremington Quay Café and Heritage Centre (free entry), housed in the former railway station. This explains the maritime, industrial and railway history of the area with period photographs and tableaux. Follow the Tarka Trail over the old railway bridge. If the tide is high, continue ahead on the cycle path. Otherwise, turn right PUBLIC FOOTPATH. Walk past the old limekilns and turn left along the foreshore, but keep clear of the unstable low cliffs. Look out for waders and wildfowl, which find rich feeding on the estuary mud. The path continues to Salt Pill Duck Pond and beyond, but note dogs are not allowed into this small nature reserve.

Walk 15 Saunton Sands

The great sweep of Saunton Sands makes one of Devon's finest beach walks – up to 6km of golden sand. Take off your shoes and stroll along the water's edge and explore the massive dune system, Braunton Burrows, which is noted for its rich variety of wildflowers, butterflies and birds. It covers 750ha (1800 acres) and is a key part of North Devon's UNESCO Biosphere Reserve. Please note that whilst the public is generally very welcome on the Burrows, part is also used as a military training area. On rare occasions, red flags

A pond within the dunes of Saunton Sands

The path between Croyde and Baggy Point

are flown and this area is closed for live firing. You may see soldiers or military vehicles – keep out of their way and don't touch any debris.

Walk 16 Croyde to Baggy Point

The 1.6 km (1 mile) walk along a broad, smooth path from the National Trust car park in Croyde at SS 433397 is amply rewarded with superb views. Baggy Point is an SSSI (Site of Special Scientific Interest) because of its varied birdlife, including colonies of gulls, raptors and larks, as well as its fascinating shale and sandstone geology. Look out for some enormous bones beside the path. They are the remains of a whale washed up in 1915.

Walk 17 Heddon's Mouth Cleave

A beautiful level path, 1.7 km (1 mile) long, links the National Trust car park and the beach at Heddon's Mouth. Cut by a fast-flowing river, Heddon's Mouth Cleave is a steep sided valley lined by towering cliffs rising to 248 m (818 ft). Turn left out of the car park and left in front of Hunter's Inn, COMBE MARTIN BARNSTAPLE. After 300 m, turn right, HEDDON'S MOUTH. Simply ignore all side turnings and follow the path to the beach. Retrace your steps for 200 m. Turn left over the footbridge and follow the river back to Hunter's Inn.

Walk 18 Woody Bay

Park carefully close to a hairpin bend on the lane leading down from Martinhoe to Woody Bay at SS 674487 (please do not block the entrance to the path) – or leave your car in the car park at SS 675445 and follow the lane downhill. Follow PUBLIC FOOTPATH HUNTER'S INN. This former carriage drive is broad and near level. Fine views open out through the trees and along the coast to the Valley of Rocks. You may wish to walk on for 2 km (1 1/4 miles) to visit the Roman fortlet, which is signed on the left up a narrow path.

Opposite: Heddon's Mouth

Right: View over Woody Bay

The dramatic Valley of Rocks, a site of great geological interest

Walk 19   Lynton North Walk and the Valley of Rocks

An easy 2 km (1¼ miles) walk along the level and well-surfaced North Walk gives wonderful coastal views and leads to the extraordinary Valley of Rocks. Now a dry valley, it was the former course of the Lyn, a powerful river which left considerable deposits of rock behind. The valley was further eroded by glacial action. Such action was exceptional in Devon, which lay at the southern extremity of the ice sheets that covered most of Britain during the last Ice Age.

Walk 20 Lynmouth to Watersmeet

The 3 km (2 mile) bankside walk along the East Lyn to the National Trust tea room, shop and information centre at Watersmeet is an Exmoor classic, with the river rushing over tumbled boulders in its steep, densely wooded valley. The path is well surfaced and well graded and walkers have the choice of using bridges to explore either bank for much of the way. Beautiful at any time, it is doubly so after rain when the East Lyn roars over tumbled boulders and its several waterfalls are supercharged.

   Please beware of slippery rocks and avoid this walk after very heavy rain – the river rises extremely fast and can be dangerous. Start from Lynmouth's Lyndale Cross car park. Cross the road bridge at the lower end. Turn right along Tors Road and uphill, parallel to the river. After 100 m, bear right through a public garden and simply follow the riverbank path to Watersmeet.